Dog Training

A Thorough Contemporary Guide For Nurturing Your Pet With Affection And Comprehension Acquire All The Essential Knowledge On Properly Raising Your Dog

(A Comprehensive And Detailed Guide On The Process Of Training A Dog To Follow Commands With Discipline)

Mariano Fitzpatrick

TABLE OF CONTENT

Canine Psychology 1

Phobias And Fear 8

Additional Assistance With Separation Anxiety Training..20

The Dutch Shepherd: Its History And Qualities 57

How To Teach Obedience Effectively 83

Reckless Dog 111

Stop Troublesome Conduct Before It Occurs. 111

An Immediate Overview Of Dog Training................ 140

Canine Psychology

As previously said, dogs live in packs and regard their owners as leaders or Alpha males rather than as pals. Humans are fallible in this situation and do not set boundaries or limits. For instance, most dog owners release their devoted companions from their homes. They allow their dog to sleep wherever in the house and allow them to eat anywhere in the house. Without realizing the true significance of the dog's bark, people feed them food if they bark for any other cause. When dogs yell at them, they don't halt to appease the commotion. Humans only act in certain ways, such as those seen in the cases above, either out of ignorance or because they regard dogs like people.

The question at hand is how to solve the psychological issue with dogs. I'd want to start by outlining the distinction between dog training and psychology. It is untrue that some trainers claim that they are two distinct things. You may easily train your dog to meet your needs if they are psychologically balanced. Dog behavior is closely influenced by dog psychology, which makes training a dog's behavior crucial. For instance, your training efforts will be in vain if your dog exhibits behavioral issues since they will never comprehend your directions. In order to resolve these problems, we must first examine canine psychological problems and potential solutions.

Dogs often have a few typical psychological problems.

Obsessive-compulsive disorder

This is the most prevalent psychological problem that adult and puppy dogs face. In this instance, the dog begins to exhibit the same behaviors regularly, such as tail-chasing, chasing shadows and reflections, excessive licking, etc.

Reasons

This type of psychological issue is brought on by stress, worry, etc. There is no difficulty in solving this issue. All you need to do is stop your dog from acting this way. For example, you only need to divert your dog from chasing his tail if he does it regularly. Anything can be used as a distraction. Use a leash, food, or anything else that interests your dog. Just keep drawing his attention away from that specific task. Continue doing this until the behavior starts to alter.

Uncertainty

Dogs can exhibit a variety of anxiety disorders if individuals believe that anxiety is limited to tension, despair, or terror. No, it is incorrect. Even if the causes might be the same, things are different in the world of dogs. Separation anxiety is a prevalent anxiety in the dog world. It is easily detected in dogs, even in their adult years. It occurs due to the close bonds that dogs form with their owners, mates, or companions. Furthermore, undue affection and attention can sometimes lead to worry.

You may find it strange, yet this is a fact. You have to have witnessed this in people as well. Just as an overly protective girlfriend may occasionally become unpleasant, taking extra care of their kids can occasionally cause tension. Similar situations arise in the world of dogs. Sometimes, a dog owner gets so protective of their pet that they won't even let them walk or do anything on their own. Dogs who have this kind of relationship experience tension and anxiety.

The type of anxiety a dog has will undoubtedly affect how they are treated. Initially, the owner must determine if the dog is acting out because of separation anxiety or refusing your love and care. Toys, puzzles that need constant play, marrowbones, or anything else that holds his attention for an extended period can all help reduce separation anxiety. Take note of the anxiety time as you repeat this procedure if the dog uses these items and displays no signs of nervousness. Try to extend the process until the dog gets rid of all nervousness.

Reducing the owner's bond with the dog is one possible treatment for affection anxiety. When you are driving or leaving the house, try to avoid it. Ignorance can give a dog reason to consider your actions and attempt to reclaim your bond. You can remove restrictions and boundaries during this time to help your dog overcome his fear.

Phobias And Fear

It is primarily present in fancy or toy breeds and is particular to certain environments, objects, or circumstances. Fear, ignorance, drooling, hunger, needless violence, running away, and lethargy are some of the symptoms.

A traumatic incident led to the development of these phobias and fears. As I mentioned earlier, dogs are good at building relationships because they can relate to people and understand emotions. A dog may suffer from a negative event. However, an owner's out-of-balance response might exacerbate the damage, making the dog perceive the situation as dangerous and fearful.

Due to negative experiences, the dog still has the most of its phobia. For instance, suppose a dog gets into a car accident and hears tire noises just before the collision. He might be terrified of that noise for the rest of his life.

There's just one way out of these problems: to face your fear. For instance, if you support the dog when he is afraid, he will see you as a helping hand. With your assistance, he could confront his fear and return to normal after the fresh experience clears his memory.

Solving Separation Anxiety Problems

Suppose your adult or puppy dog is exhibiting what seem to be clinical symptoms of moderate to severe separation anxiety. In that case, you will probably need to look into expert interventions in addition to more advanced and targeted training techniques. Even though separation anxiety affects extremely few domestic dogs, a dog with separation anxiety will nevertheless cause challenges for you and your family. If untreated, this may result in persistent behavioral issues and health issues.

These approaches can help reduce symptoms if your puppy or adult dog exhibits unpleasant behaviors, such as excessive property destruction, fearfulness, barking, whimpering, whining, or anxiety. If any of these traits are present in your dog, it's feasible that they will improve mental health and exhibit calmer mannerisms if you take proactive steps and work together. Eliminating the negative impact of SA on your pet will also significantly enhance your emotional well-being.

Some basic dog training methods can help with minor anxiety symptoms.

● Save your dog from being bored. Provide lots of chew toys, age-appropriate physical exercise for at least 30 minutes each day, one or two obedience training sessions per day, and socialization sessions.

● Before your scheduled absence, engage in some physical activity, such as a quick game of fetch or brisk walk, to burn off any extra energy that would otherwise exacerbate anxiety during your absence.

● You can distract or soothe him while you're away by turning on a low-volume radio or television. Try it out first to be sure your puppy is soothed rather than agitated before proceeding.

● Fill your alone time with plush toys. These toys can be packed so that it takes him a long time to remove the food, keeping him occupied for extended periods. One wonderful thing about these chew toys is that they cannot bark, whine, or cry when they are being chewed on.

Moderate symptoms might be more severe than the characteristics of mild anxiety and require more intense behavioral modification strategies. Resolving the problem may take weeks or months and require daily practice through focused dog training.

● To begin with, boost the amount of activity your Koolie puppy receives daily while staying within the suggested boundaries. Ensure your small puppy doesn't overheat, and if he belongs to an extra-large breed, watch out that he doesn't jump or do anything else that could harm his developing bones.

Start several intense workout routines each day that involve games, fast walks, and two to three fetch game sessions if you can. If your dog isn't interested in fetch, try another game or kind of exercise that will get his heart rate up and burn off some energy. Aim for two or more 30-minute activity-based intervals per day at the very least.

It is recommended to conduct two 10-minute training sessions every day to master the fundamental commands, followed by teaching sit-stay or down-stay. Sit and down-stay commands are excellent for building your dog's self-confidence so he may be left alone. Teach him to tolerate being apart from you in various settings and times.

● When he is old enough and has had at least his first set of vaccinations, it is another fantastic choice. By doing this, he will improve his social skills and gain confidence under the supervision of a qualified expert. These courses teach people how to engage and train their puppies as well.

● It's critical that you work on progressively widening the distance between you and your dog if you have a

"Shadow dog," which is a dog that will not leave your side. This is simple to accomplish by gradually lengthening the time you are apart from him and using his cage or gated area as his isolation place.

You should release him from his confines when you observe a lull in his worrying or when you start with little intervals of time apart. Make sure not to create a huge deal from his release from his limitations; instead, act as if it were simply another ordinary day. If your dog continues to exhibit destructive tendencies or gets very agitated in isolation settings, especially in his crate, then take extra care and make the necessary adjustments. If so, don't use his crate for this specific training session. We want our puppies to adore their crates and see them as a secure refuge.

Another technique to help your dog overcome his separation anxiety issues is desensitizing him to your absence. Even seemingly insignificant actions, like reaching for your coat or bag or hearing the sound of keys clinking, can occasionally cause your puppy to become agitated in anticipation of your departure.

● If your puppy is still too attached to you for you to leave them, start by pretending to be leaving the house. Perform the necessary actions, like getting your briefcase or house keys, but instead of leaving, simply carry your belongings around the house for a short while before putting them away.

Try this three to five times a day until you no longer see your dog seeming agitated or apprehensive when you are making your pretend departure arrangements. Dog-to-dog differences exist in how long this training takes to be successful. Training your dog may take a day, a few days, a week, or even longer, depending on him and his temperament.

- Proceed to the following stage: exit the premises and repeat the previous process. Start by briefly going outside and then coming back inside. Gradually extend the time you wait outside your home before returning inside during this training. The secret is to always seem as though leaving or returning home is not a significant occasion deserving of celebration. Just get your belongings and head off. Maintain this training until your dog gets less agitated by your frequent coming and departure.

● After a long walk, step inside and return to your routine, giving your dog no attention for at least five to ten minutes. When you're ready to show your dog some love and affection, or give him what he deserves after this period.

How to minimize your dog's symptoms before you depart

1. Take your dog for a quick, brisk walk or a hard workout.

2. To reduce feelings of loneliness, switch on the television or radio if this has shown to be calming rather than upsetting.

3. Give him lots of things to occupy his time.

4. Quickly depart without expressing any strong feelings for your dog.

Additional Assistance With Separation Anxiety Training

1. Get a dog walker or pet sitter to come by at least once daily.

2. Find out from your neighbors how your Dog behaves when you're not home.

3. Drop your Dog off at a doggie daycare once or twice weekly.

4. If none of the dog training advice in this guide seems to be helping, get assistance from a professional trainer and consult your veterinarian.

5. If you've exhausted all other options and still can't get your Dog to settle down, some drugs can assist. I advise using this as a stopgap measure as part of holistic therapy. At the same time, you continue to use the strategies and tactics mentioned to mold and modify your Dog's behavior. If you give your dog medication, look for the safest natural remedy or follow your veterinarian's instructions.

6. Don't crate your Dog for extended periods.

7. Refrain from penalizing events or accidents due to SA. Recall that a dog suffering from SA lacks self-control due to the ingrained nature of his issue. For instance, as seen by the soiling of things connected to his fears.

Having a happy, healthy, and well-adjusted dog who can handle any situation that comes his way is the ultimate goal and result of this training. As stated earlier, prevention of separation anxiety can provide you with the comfort of knowing that you won't have to endure this demanding training and that you won't have to put up with the irritation of constant whimpering, barking, gnawing, and tearing. Other behaviors associated with doggie anxiety will hurt you, your family, visiting friends, and your neighbors.

Only 10 to 15 percent of domestic dog owners report that their pets experience separation anxiety to some extent.

Fortunately, it is not too difficult to stop abnormal barking when it is problematic.

Avoidance at Home with a Clicker

Teaching your American Akita to be quiet is the first step toward teaching them not to bark. Using the order "Quiet" to your dog when you are at home can help stop him from barking. Tell him to be quiet the moment he begins to bark. Put a treat in front of his nose. Click your clicker and give him the treat as a reward when he stops sniffing it. Repeat after him, rewarding him for every few seconds of silence. He'll discover that remaining silent earns him goodies. In the future, when he becomes silent following a trigger, don't forget to reward him. In due course, he will learn to be silent and to follow "Quiet." And eventually, the practice of remaining silent will win out over the habit of barking.

In order to stop him from barking, you must act assertively if he disobeys your order to be quiet. Aim to block the stimulus causing him distress. Utilize the time-out technique to remove him from the stimulus for a short time and educate him that barking equates to being confined alone and unable to see and investigate everything happening.

Preventing Outside of the House

Fido is silent, so you cannot click to reward him when you are away from home and have not brought him along. It's something you want to do to stop him from barking when you're not around.

Start by attempting to eliminate as many stimuli as you can. For example, if your American Akita enjoys barking at the mailman, you should shut the drapes to prevent him from seeing the street.

It's humane to use a citronella spray collar to teach him that barking is associated with the bad scent of citronella, which dogs detest. When he barks, this collar will activate and spray him. He'll pick up silence fairly soon.

Additional Bark Prevention While Committing Together

Training your American Akita to control his excessive barking when you take him for walks or driving is possible.

At home, begin by teaching him to "Watch me." Put something sweet to your nose and say, "Observe me." Click and present the treat to him when he looks at it. Ten to fifteen repetitions will help it form a new, virtuous habit. After that, extend the wait period to two or three seconds to ensure he glances at the treat. Repeat this process twelve times. Lastly, teach him that this motion indicates "watch me" by holding a pretend treat up to your nose. Once you reach fifteen seconds, keep increasing the times.

Start using this command outside your home before you go out in public. Continue to keep him away from anything that can cause him to bark. Give him fifteen seconds to gaze at you, and then give him a treat and a click.

Tell him to "Watch me" now that you are out in public to divert his focus from whatever he barks at. To teach him that this motion means to watch you, try holding the pretend reward up to your nose. Present him with a treat when he looks at you. He'll eventually learn to look at you and not bark when you two go out.

If your Dog barks at certain stimuli, you might also try this command. Hold the imaginary goodie up to your nose and give him the "Watch me" instruction whenever he starts to bark. Every time he barks, teach him to turn his focus elsewhere.

If his barking is still uncontrollable, it might be time to use a citronella spray collar. You can wear it when you take him for walks outside or when you know he will likely bark. Ideally, you'll be able to teach him to just bark at the slightest hint of a treat being held to your face. He should cease barking only by making the gesture.

Preventive measures when your adorable American Akita becomes bored

Keeping your American Akita from being bored is the only method to prevent them from barking out of boredom. You want to instill in him the habit of keeping himself occupied with toys, food, and exercise. Give your American Akita at least 30 minutes a day of exercise. Play games that will challenge your mind with him. Give him something to occupy his time, such as buried goodies or a Kong filled with peanut butter, if you have to leave him inside the home or in the yard for prolonged periods.

Avoid Nipping

Playing with your American Akita puppy while carrying a chew toy will help you instill in him that biting your hands, your body, or the bodies of others is not acceptable, even at a young age. Reacting negatively when he bites the chew toy will teach him that doing so is okay. Say

"Ouch!" if he nips your hand." and turn to leave. If he wants to continue playing with you, he will learn not to nip you and be upset that playtime is finished.

You must employ restriction to make him associate nibbling with being put in a time-out if simply walking away doesn't work to educate him not to nip. When he nips, tell him to "time out" and lead him to his designated space. Tie him up on a two-foot lead for five minutes and ignore him.

Instruct your children and other family members to avoid being nipped. He interprets their flight as a challenge to pursue them. Show them how to say "Ouch!" or simply hold their ground. And turn to leave without sprinting, laughing, or yelling.

Teach him to eat with grace as well. Give him the command to be "polite." Tell him to be courteous when you feed him.

When he accepts the meal nicely, reward him. Take away the food, and don't feed it if he tries to nibble.

One effective method to help your American Akita overcome his nipping is to keep him busy. Nipping can be a serious issue, particularly if your American Akita is a puppy undergoing teething. To keep his mouth occupied, give him abundant chew toys and bones. Teach him that while he can chew on those toys, he is not allowed to chew on you or others.

Not pursuing

Naturally, your American Akita will want to pursue objects they see as prey. You can just teach him the "Watch me" command described in the barking part to get him to focus on you rather than the prey he wants to chase down. This will teach him to stop chasing any form of prey.

You may also train him not to pursue after animals using a treat and a clicker. Tell him to sit or to observe you if he starts to pursue you. To get his attention, reward him. Click to give him something to gaze at as he looks at you. He gets rewarded for listening to you, so soon, he will learn to quit chasing animals.

In situations where your American Akita will not listen, the time-out method works well. Take him away from his target and restrain him for five minutes. Continue doing this even if you tell him no and he still pursues you.

Make sure your Dog understands that you are calling for him. He must follow your instructions, especially if he feels tempted to pursue something or someone. In the following chapter, I'll discuss instruction that demands greater debt.

It's crucial to wear a leash whenever your Dog is outside. His powerful chasing impulse will not be easily broken or instantaneously activated. You must keep your Dog on an appropriate leash outside your home to protect him, other animals, and your neighbors.

Early exposure to cats and other pets will teach your Dog to view these creatures as friends rather than potential food sources or prey. He will acquire an appreciation for other creatures through repeated exposure and interactions.

No Retreating

If your Dog escapes, it could cause you a lot of problems or, even worse, harm or even death. When your American Akita gets bored or notices anything, like a rabbit or deer, you want to train him not to rush away.

One effective strategy to prevent your Dog from running away is to spay or neuter them when they are young. Dogs typically flee in search of a partner. Should you decide to breed your pet instead of neutering or spaying him or her, you may want to keep him or her indoors during the heat. You should always walk your American Akita on a leash and keep him in a gated yard where he can't tunnel under or jump over to get out. Dogs will do anything to locate a hot date in heat. Also thrown away are appearances.

Reward your Dog when he returns home if he runs away and returns on his own. Tell him you adore him. If he goes out again, he will desire to stay home and always return. The main objective is to keep your Dog from running away to protect him and any people or their pets he might encounter when he is outside your fence in the wild.

Absence of Aggression

It is never acceptable to act aggressively. There are several reasons why your Dog might turn violent. Making it plain that aggression will never be directed toward you or others, nor will it be accepted in situations that do not pose a threat, is the best way to deal with it.

Being non-aggressive and maintaining composure is the initial step. Maintain your position. Never give up, or you'll instill in your American Akita the belief that he is in charge, not you. Show him you are in control, and he should not be hostile toward you.

Teach your Dog to go to his box when the doorbell rings or something else triggers his violent behavior. To begin, ring the doorbell (or show him whatever triggers his aggression), lure him inside his box, and reward him with a goodie. Educate him to use the clicker anytime his trigger appears while he is in your house, and then educate him to link it with going to his crate. Give him praise and goodies as he enters his crate. When he begins to feel scared or agitated, it helps that the crate is his haven where he can unwind.

In addition, time-outs might be necessary if your American Akita starts acting aggressively toward others. Tell him no when he behaves aggressively and put him in his time-out area on a short lead for five minutes or until he settles down and stops growling. He'll discover that he has to be by himself and away from the scene when he acts aggressively. He will want to quit acting aggressively to stay in the room with you and yours.

If your Dog acts aggressively because he is terrified, consider rewarding him with a treat and guiding him away from the source of his anxiety. Approach his worries with caution and expose him to them gradually. Talk to him in a kind, gentle tone and comfort him. He will learn to trust that you are the one who will always put things right and that his worries are unjustified.

When he remains composed in the face of one of his triggers for aggressiveness, make sure to lavish him with praise. You wish to instill in him the virtue of composure. He deserves praise and treats when he doesn't act aggressively and stays calm.

Taking care of your puppy's food and toys as you wish is a terrific trick. From an early age, teach him that you get to handle his belongings. When you touch something he believes to be his, he is not permitted to act very possessively. He will come to terms with you tampering with his belongings and learn to be non-aggressive.

We further detail training your Dog and rewarding positive behavior in the following two chapters. Continue reading to train your friend to be a nice dog.

Wintertime temperature changes from indoors to outdoors can result in dry, flaky skin. Throughout the winter, brushing your Dog promotes health and any potential dead hair.

Summertime:

The only way your administration hound sweats is through their footstack. Dogs cool themselves by gasping and often have trouble maintaining a sufficient internal temperature during the intense summer heat. Recognize that warmth may affect their desire to work because they may feel uncomfortable.

Some dogs, just like in the winter, don't realize that it's never safe to be outside again during the middle of the year. Some dogs will go around until they get too hot, so you must watch them and ensure they come inside before they get sick.

As they aid in keeping a dog hydrated on a hot day, they always provide easy access to water. Even more exciting treats can be added to the water by adding ice cubes in three-dimensional form, which will help them stay cool. Small plastic kiddie pools can be a great way for some dogs to relax and have fun. Avoid letting your Dog consume excessive amounts of water, which may cause heaving or swelling.

During the mid-year, the asphalt outdoors reaches high temperatures, which can cause a dog to devour its cushions. If you can comfortably hold your turn in touch with the blacktop for ten seconds, it's a good general rule of thumb. After that, it's safe for your Dog. When it becomes unbearably hot for you, it also becomes unbearably hot for your dog. Make a concerted effort to stop close to buildings during the late spring to minimize the time your Dog must travel on asphalt when available instead of the walkway in front of you.

In the late spring, booties can withstand extremely high temperatures quite well.

It is advised that strolls be held for around ten to fifteen minutes if the temperature is above eighty degrees.

Mutts can practice walking this distance without getting too hot.

Dogs' Perception

You may manipulate an image that you transmit to see how a dog might see the same situation, thanks to a website called Dog Vision.

What are the noteworthy differences? Taking everything into account, there are many.

Their perception of shading differs from ours. Because each of the three colors has sensitive receptors in the eyes, people can perceive red, green, and blue. But the cells that read red and green are the same in hounds. Thus, it's harder to distinguish between the two colors. This theory contradicts the recently accepted but disproved belief that dogs could not see color at all. They can see a few hues despite having a limited range and not being able to judge a shading's excellence the same way that people can. Examine the Dog Vision-created outline below to consider both their and our range.

Dogs' Odor

The sense of smell in mutts surpasses that of humans by orders of magnitude; it is 10,000 to many times more potent. Dogs can only detect a few parts per trillion of a fragrance.

Furthermore, compared to our minds, the portion of a dog's brain devoted to identifying scents is far more prominent. Furthermore, mutts' noses function differently from ours. When we inhale, our noses use comparable flight paths to detect scent and inhale. A fold of tissue within the noses of mutts separates these two functions at inhalation. According to Pennsylvania State University bioengineer Brent Craven, "we found that when wind current enters the nose, it parts into two distinctive stream ways, one for olfaction and one for breath."

People's sense of smell is limited to a small region on top of the nasal depression, located along the main path of wind flow. Thus, when we unwind, the air we smell enters and exits. About 12 percent of the aroused air in hounds goes via a slanted area at the back of the nose used for smell, with the remaining air clearing beyond that niche and disappearing into the pharynx and lungs. The stench-filled air passes through a labyrinth of hard, scroll-like structures called turbinates inside the recessed zone.

Let's Start with the Fundamentals

Dogs and all humans in the home are required to act appropriately. If they are acting in the way that is expected of them, everyone in the house will benefit. Dogs typically seek human approval. Since dogs genuinely want to please us, educating them on what is expected will undoubtedly make them feel good about themselves when they fulfill requests. In addition to housebreaking, additional forms of training should be prioritized and deemed vital for all dogs to acquire. Enjoy the company of your dog and teach them basic obedience. Conversely, a dog lacking obedience skills can cause much trouble. Basic orders that your dog should be able to obey include these.

1. Sit – This aids in your dog's control in various circumstances. Additionally, it's one of the simplest tricks to teach a dog.

To teach a puppy to sit, get down on their level. You can take a seat in a chair or on the floor. ● Holding a treat in your hand. Make sure you repeat this each day with consistency. To ensure that your German Shepherd understands your instructions, always use the word "sit."

Don't forget to hold the treat low enough so the puppy can't jump for it. Raise it just far enough for him to extend his neck. Say "nice sit!" to him whenever his butt touches the ground. Although you can perform this repeatedly, your dog will become weary. Completing it quickly multiple times a day. Practice getting him to sit before placing his food bowl on the ground.

2. Come – This trains the dog to come to you immediately when you give the command. This command should be taught to the puppy as soon as he learns his name. This can shield your puppy from possible danger. This is also a big aid in controlling the obnoxious characteristics and behaviors of the puppy.

How to instruct a come:

After the puppy becomes used to having a line attached to him, take up the end and hold it while you follow him. ● Attach a light line to his collar and let him drag it around. Your dog will eventually grasp and comprehend that the two of you are bonded to one another as he grows used to it. Then, move backward while urging him to follow you. Say "Yes!" as soon as he approaches you, and offer him a treat. Give him lots of praise and the impression that he's the world's smartest dog.

● Every time you give an order, always say "come." Reward and commend the dog each time he responds appropriately.

Never develop the habit of repeatedly yelling at your dog to "come, come, come" when they don't reply. Never forget the maxim "One word, one command." Go to your dog and be nice when he understands but refuses to come when you ask. Point him in the direction you want him to go. You should also remember that calling your dog in for punishment is inappropriate. If that occurs, you are forcing him to associate the command with a bad situation. It is usually preferable to confront a misbehaving dog face-to-face instead of calling him to come inside.

3. Down: This is an excellent tool for training and helping to keep your puppy out of danger. Since the down behavioris

an act of surrender, it can be challenging to teach puppies. A timid and anxious puppy may find it more difficult to learn the down, so constantly speak upbeat, seem content, give lots of praise and goodies, and most importantly, have the patience to go slowly.

● Get a tempting treat, hold it in your closed hand, and point it at the puppy's muzzle. ● Once the puppy notices the fragrance of the reward, move your hand to the floor. This is how you teach Down. He'll follow the hand that has the treat hidden.

● Move your hand before the dog when his head follows yours while holding the treat. When you observe him stretching downward, you should open his hand

and let him consume the food inside. ●
Repeat this several times a day. You will notice that his body follows his head. Use the word "down" at all times.

Once the dog learns the fundamentals, it will become easier to handle and more enjoyable. You will both be content and have a wonderful, enjoyable relationship.

dietary aggression

The most crucial thing to remember in this situation is that you will need to retrain and recondition your dog, and you should never punish him for being aggressive with food.

First, establish a strict feeding schedule that you follow. Feed your dog twice or three times a day; do not always keep the food bowls filled. Don't forget to give your dog the same amount of food each time.

Your dog will feel less tempted to guard the food and will instead perceive you as the one in control of it, waiting for you to feed him if he recognizes you as the source of his food. Feed your dog in a different room to eradicate any sense of ownership he may have towards the feeding spot. Furthermore, feed every other animal from the newly created feeding area separately from your dog.

Hostility Towards Other Dogs

Another common source of dog aggression is antagonism towards other dogs. One technique to help your dogs get to know one another if you have more than one dog in the house is to take them for walks while each is wearing a leash.

If you have multiple dogs and they have been friends for some time, they may be fighting because they don't have a clear alpha leader. You will have to take on this leadership role in this situation. You can disprove any hostile behavior between the dogs in your home by exhibiting alpha leadership.

Don't Give up on Rewarding Behavior

All dog owners must understand that aggression in and of itself should never be encouraged, nor should it be tolerated. For this reason, if your dog exhibits hostility toward someone, make sure that you abstain from providing positive reinforcement, like patting or consoling him. Such conduct will only be reinforced by such acts.

Plus, you really should not chastise your dog. This may confuse your dog and make things worse. Instead of reacting to your dog's behavior, your main goal should be improving it.

By this point, you need to discern that multiple triggers exist for canines to exhibit aggressive conduct and that there are numerous ways to counteract the undesirable behavior. The most crucial aspect of helping your dog overcome this bad behavior is to act unwaveringly and exhibit strong alpha leadership traits while teaching them obedience training methods.

How To Stop Being Aggressive

Always remember that options and fixes are accessible to help you control your dog during training. The first thing to do is to take your dog to the vet to ensure everything is well and that there is no reason for him to act aggressively.

The second thing you need to do is ensure your dog wears the appropriate muzzles and leashes in public areas. Finally, learn to minimize some experiences, including passing by another dog or observing a dog or person approach you and your dog.

It's important to keep in mind that your dog can sense your anxiety and thrive on it, especially if they're wearing a leash or other form of restraint, which could make things worse. The foundation of behavior training is still an alpha leadership and stability relationship between you and your dog; once this is established, training will be easier to handle.

Training Methods for Success: Because Dutch Shepherds are intelligent and like to please people, they are naturally trainable. Unlocking their full potential, however, requires a combination of disciplined training methods, positive reinforcement, and consistency. The main goals of behavioral training and obedience instruction should be to prevent bad behaviors, establish excellent manners, and set clear boundaries and expectations.

What Makes Early Socialization Important?

Early socialization is essential to raising a well-rounded Dutch Shepherd who gets along well with kids, strangers, and other animals. Exposing them to a range of situations, people, and stimuli may help them become more self-assured, reduce any concerns they may have, and develop close relationships with both humans and animals.

Adopting or Buying a Dutch Shepherd: It's important to consider their energy levels, exercise needs, and the difficulties of their independent and protective character before deciding whether to adopt or buy one. To give this amazing breed a happy and loving forever home, be sure your lifestyle and living arrangements can meet their requirements.

The Dutch Shepherd: Its History And Qualities

The Dutch Shepherd is a unique medium-to-large dog breed that originated in the Netherlands and has a long history of working with farmers and shepherds. They make excellent working dogs and well-known pets due to their intelligence, agility, and adaptability.

Dutch Shepherds are renowned for their loyalty and protectiveness and have a close bond with their owners. Thanks to their well-balanced temperament, they perform well in various jobs, including law enforcement, competitive athletics, and search and rescue operations. They are a great option for anyone looking for a flexible canine companion because of their adaptability and readiness to please.

There are three different types of this dense double coat on these amazing dogs: short, long, and rough hair. Nonetheless, their remarkable brindle coloring is an unquestionable characteristic that distinguishes them from other breeds. Their striking appearance draws attention everywhere they go because of their distinctive striped pattern.

Comprehending a Dutch Shepherd's urges and instincts to teach and socialize them appropriately is crucial. Due to their innate tendencies and working history, owners must provide them with mental stimulation and organized instruction. Using their intelligence and motivation to accomplish desired behaviors requires patience, consistency, and positive reinforcement.

Because they require constant mental and physical stimulation, owners who are sedentary or inactive should not keep Dutch Shepherds. These active dogs flourish when their endless energy is given something to do. Their minds are kept active and satisfied with difficult activities, interactive play sessions, and regular exercise.

Despite being a typically healthy breed, Dutch Shepherds can have inherited eye problems, allergies, and hip dysplasia, among other diseases. Preventive treatment, a healthy diet, and routine veterinary exams are essential to preserving their general health.

Dutch Shepherds are highly trainable, showing their intellect and desire to learn. On the other hand, a systematic approach, consistency, and positive reinforcement are necessary for effective training. Behavioral training and obedience should be continuous endeavors, even with a well-trained dog.

A fully-rounded Dutch Shepherd that gets along well with kids, strangers, and other animals is developed through early socialization. Early socialization with various people, places, and animals is crucial for molding their behavior and guaranteeing that they develop into self-assured, gregarious canines.

Adopting or buying a Dutch Shepherd should be done with much care and deliberation. Compared to more sedentary breeds, they have higher energy levels and exercise requirements. Thus, they need a committed owner who can provide for their needs. Their independent and protective personality necessitates skilled handling and proactive instruction to properly handle potential obstacles.

Chapter 8: Training at Home

The first significant challenge for new dog owners is frequent house training. The fundamentals of training dogs stay the same whether they are newborn puppies or mature canines: constancy, tolerance, and positive reward. Nevertheless, depending on your dog's age, there are some subtle differences in approach. Now, let's explore it.

Dogs: Puppies versus Adults

Your dog's age greatly influences how quickly and easily they learn to potty train. Puppies typically need more frequent trips and have poorer bladder control. Although adult dogs may have received some training already, they may also need to break negative habits.

Puppies in Training at Home

Regular toilet Breaks: Puppies need frequent breaks due to their small bladders and rapid metabolisms.

Crate Training: Using a crate can assist in controlling a puppy's bowel habits and lowering accidents.

Positive Reinforcement: When your puppy goes outside to relieve themselves, always give them praise and treats.

Accident Prevention: Mishaps are inevitable. Remove any fragrance indicators that can entice your dog to return to the area by thoroughly cleaning it.

Adult Dogs Being House Trained

Examine Past Training: While older dogs may already be somewhat housebroken, they may require a fresh start if they have spent a lot of time in shelters or were outdoor dogs.

Establish Routine: Just like puppies, adult dogs thrive on structure. House training will be easier if you feed and walk them simultaneously daily.

Using command words such as "Go potty" can assist your dog in associating the behavior with the term.

Positive Reinforcement: Positive conduct deserves rewards, even in mature dogs. Make good use of rewards and compliments.

Solving House Training Problems

Some issues come up with dogs of any age, whether puppies or adults.

Refusal to Go Outside: Owing to fear or bad experiences in the past, a dog may occasionally refuse to go outside. Slow desensitization can be beneficial.

Certain dogs mark their territory indoors. This issue can be lessened by eliminating the smell and changing the behavior.

Housebreaking a pet might be one of the most difficult jobs for novice pet owners, but it's also one of the most important for a peaceful home. No matter how old your dog is, persistence and patience are essential.

How I Got to Be My "Pack's" Leader

I created this eBook for three reasons. I had to help you see why you should become the dominant dog in your household. However, I also wanted to support you in trying to, at least partially, view the world through your dog's eyes. Finally, I needed to help you start thinking more like your dog instead of expecting her to think the same as you!

After all, we can successfully adjust situational and willingly alter our behavior to fit different situations. We understand that every action has consequences. These are essentially things that your dog is incapable of.

And because that's the way things stand, you have to become the dominant dog, take charge, and provide her with the stable pack environment she desires for the duration of her life.

Ideally, you should start doing the exercises I will teach you when your dog is still a small puppy, between three and four months old. Don't panic, though, if your dog is older than that. Candy was almost two years old when I finally realized that my lack of knowledge was the biggest challenge we would have to overcome!

You know the adage, "You can't teach new habits when the old ones are so deeply ingrained"? Considering everything, Candy and I are living proof that's just not the case!

The First Steps to Developing Into a Successful Pack Leader

There's ONE really important thing you want to do before I walk you through how to prepare for your alpha canine.

Establish Your Home's Regulations!

Bonus Advice: Make sure you complete it together! Include every family member so that everyone agrees on how you will care for your dog.

Recall that when your dog does anything wrong, it will be easier to enforce the standards if everyone knows them!

Additionally, after your House Rules are documented in writing, you'll need to incorporate the following several items into your routine:

I stress this enough: consistency is essential. You must always treat your dog fairly, no matter what! No exceptions!

Don't wait to enforce your house rules after you bring your puppy home—that's a BIG mistake!

Stay composed but firm at all times. Avoid enforcing your house rules when you're upset or fatigued.

Never scold or strike your dog.

Remember to never reward your dog for any aggressive or scary behaviors.

Treats can be used to promote appropriate conduct in addition to affection and praise (at least in the beginning)

Now that we have established these priorities let's start by looking at the fundamentals of how you can demonstrate strength every day.

What You'll Need Is This

Energetic training programs are fantastic for maintaining your dog's intellectual and physical fitness. But make sure you have a good rope and collar that fit your dog's needs before you leave for your first meeting.

There are many different kinds of chains and collars available. Additionally, bridles and leads are designed for various dog personalities, ages, and explicit situations. Speak with your local pet retailer to see which ones are appropriate for your plans for your dog's preparation.

Treats for dogs and clickers can also help your dog learn what behavior you find acceptable and what you find unacceptable.

Never Undervalue the Influence of Mentality!

You will need more than a few dog preparation exercises to handle if you genuinely want to ensure you are the burden bearer in your relationship with your dog. Your attitude plays a big role in how your dog perceives you and how quickly she will come to recognize you as the dominant dog in the pack.

While practicing the Alpha Canine Preparation exercises, remember the following important points. You'll be amazed at what you've accomplished when you make them a HABIT!

1. Your Conduct Should Be Calm But Assertive - You should be certain and persistent if you want to be in charge. Give your dog instructions, but don't give up on her if she doesn't comply. Your dog must learn that you mean business and that if you give an order, she wants to follow it. 2. Your Dog's Conduct Should Be Calm But Submissive - When preparing and caring for ropes,

make sure your dog is cooperative and quiet before allowing her to proceed with anything. Putting this guideline into practice will also make it easier to keep your dog from being overly anxious when you leave the house or when you come home after prolonged periods away.

3. The Value of Awards: We generally enjoy receiving awards occasionally. And so does your dog. Your dog will soon learn that obeying your commands is cool while you train her to sit and reward her every time she complies. You can eventually replace the treat with praise, and your dog will still follow your instructions since they will perceive your favorable regard as a treat in and of

itself. Your final goal is to get your dog straight, where following your instructions is enough.

4. The Boss Takes The Lead - You need to take the lead in many situations. While you shouldn't go out of your way to be the first to eat or enter a room, you should ensure your dog isn't taking advantage of the opportunity to walk ahead of you or take food off your plate. Keep silent. Have confidence in yourself.

5. Always Pay Attention to Your Body Language: Your dog responds to different levels of stimulation. One of the most important forms of communication you use is nonverbal! So, take a tall stance. Keep your head up. And when you talk to your dog, never back down.

It's not necessary to talk loudly or look her down. Just maintain your composure. Stay confident. And maintain control. It's amazing how much this will improve your dog's obedience to your directions.

Instruction Based on Breed

As I mentioned earlier, dogs were typically raised for employment. They were placed in sprinting, swarming, and hunting positions. As a result, they received food and water and benefited from the social standing of being a pack leader.

When getting your dog ready, you may find it helpful to learn more about her diversity.

Having a giddy dark Lab at home (like me!) or any more than 600 distinct types available makes no difference. Honestly, she wasn't raised to be the center of attention on your hallway rug or to spend her days nibbling at rawhide bones.

She is looking for growth, action, and initiative. If you give her that, she will follow and trust you to the ends of the planet!

Let's look into a few of the various dog breeds you might encounter:

Working Dogs: Canines bred specifically for a certain job are frequently called working dogs. To just a few, I'm referring to Akitas, Dobermans, Danes,

Malamutes, Mastiffs, and Rottweilers. These dogs are frequently employed for guard duty, rescue, and pulling.

The Akita is a working dog breed.

If your pet is of this type, you must give them something meaningful to keep them happy. That isn't barbaric. These dogs are happiest when they are busy! Pulling anything or pushing a dog backpack with light weights are good examples of strength-based training.

(Note: You wouldn't want to exacerbate any undiagnosed back or health issues, so schedule a quick visit with your veterinarian before doing this.)

Sporting Dogs: Originally, these outfit-wearing dogs were bred for their typical hunting abilities, including tracking and locating prey without actually killing them. Some sports breeds you might be familiar with are Weimaraners, Labradors, Golden Retrievers, Cocker Spaniels, and Setters.

The Weimaraner is a sporting dog breed.

If your dog wears a collar, swimming and fetching Frisbees are fantastic ways to help her develop her natural hunting and trailing skills. And while not every dog wearing a strange outfit is energetic, many of them are!

Hound Dogs: Hounds are frequently used to locate prey during a hunt because of their very sensitive noses and ability to ignore distracting noises, thanks to their large, floppy ears. This group includes Bloodhounds, Dachshunds, Beagles, and Bassets.

At that time, if you own a dog, you must look for exercises to keep its nose busy! Try hiding dog treats outside for your dog to find or hiding them inside a toy.

Breeds of Terriers: Originally developed to hunt and kill rodents such as mice, moles, groundhogs, and rats, terriers are intelligent small canines. They are quite impulsive and, if left alone, can get into a lot of trouble.

The Jack Russell Terrier breed of dogs

Play with your Terrier frequently, teach her some amazing tricks, and take her outside without a leash for a respectable romp in the yard to keep her out of trouble!

Little Dogs: Originally, there was just one purpose for raising little dogs.

- to take up a supporting role. Moreover, this adorable creature can encircle your heart with her soft little paw. Thus, take caution!

Breeds of Tiny Dogs: Shih Tzu Puppy

Should you wish to acquire a dog that is smaller than average, you should raise her with the same level of firmness as you would a much larger dog! You really ought to make an effort to teach her what behaviors are appropriate and inappropriate. And if you don't, it will be really easy for things to go out of hand.

So, prepare to harden your heart toward those large brown eyes and tiny, damp nose.

No matter how big (or small!) your dog is, their constant woofing, nipping, gnawing, and terrible mannerisms can all develop into severe problems that should never be disregarded!

Even while every dog and owner is different, having a basic idea of the breed you'll be preparing for can still be helpful. It will help you understand why your dog behaves the way it does in certain situations and how it might behave in others. It's important to realize that variety does not equal quality.

Regretfully, a variety's shape and characteristics usually result in "unfavorable criticism" regarding standing. Consider Pitbulls and Rottweilers. The terms "forceful" and "perilous" may immediately appear when you think of these types. However, dogs are generally not violent or terrible. Disrespect or careless planning is often the root cause of aggressive behavior. Two elements significantly influence how any dog will behave. When trained properly, Pitbulls and Rottweilers can make the best.

Friendly dogs in the city!

How To Teach Obedience Effectively

An authority on puppy training will tell you that obedience training is crucial for your puppy's well-being and convenience.

Whether you teach your puppy at home or with the help of a professional, you must actively participate in his obedience training. It is, therefore, an excellent chance for you to create a lifelong friendship with your new pet.

Puppy training can appear intimidating and time-consuming to a new puppy owner. But when you consider the advantages for both you and your dog, it's all worthwhile.

Since no one will be spending the entire day at home with his dog, if he is trained, he won't experience depression and won't weep all day. He will only become an aggressive dog or so terrified that he loses all self-worth due to such melancholy.

Examining an animal's response to various stimuli is a great approach to training puppies. This knowledge is important because you may utilize the techniques you used to train your pet to become more knowledgeable.

Since they have conducted various studies on the intricacy and versatility of canine driving and have seen great outcomes, any dog trainer will undoubtedly embrace this teaching method.

Knowing how your puppy reacts to different stimuli is essential to knowing which button to hit. You will find teaching easier if you can help your puppy develop his positive rather than negative drive.

You can't go wrong when a professional trainer is your guide because they have the knowledge and expertise to make greater sense of things. Nonetheless, it can assist you in realizing that play, the pack, predators, food, and protection influence your puppy's behavior. Each of these elements is equally significant, albeit the type of your dog may have a stronger inclination.

As a certified puppy educator, you should know that play is the primary way pups learn. Yes, this may shock you, but part of training a puppy is assuming parental duties.

Since you have assumed the job of your puppy's parent, it is also your responsibility to teach him how to play and run around. Additionally, it will support the growth of your relationship with your puppy.

You need to keep a few things in mind when you begin training your dog in good manners. If you use the appropriate training techniques, your outcome should be favorable. Put these guidelines into practice to simplify training for you and your dog.

1. Be Kind: A young dog may be highly reactive at first and unable to handle situations that are too stressful for them physically or mentally.

Even while learning usually happens rapidly, your puppy might not handle stress well or might receive too harsh training. It is always best to be stern but gentle while training a puppy because it may not learn as rapidly as it would otherwise.

1. Continue Training Briefly: Puppies require brief attention spans like children. Your dog will be more disappointed if you are careless with her because she won't know anything. Ensure your workouts are brief—ten to fifteen minutes is a reasonable time.

3. Have Patience: Puppies cannot be trained in a single day. Recognize that this cycle will take some time and maintain your attention. Remain calm and remember that pups learn in spurts and that these tasks require time.

Puppies also have severe memory impairments. If your dog appears to be missing certain training sessions daily, try not to become discouraged. You'll be fine if you have tolerance for education.

4. Make it simple: Train your puppy according to a step-by-step approach for optimal results. Compared to when you have a rigorous training regimen, your dog can learn more and more quickly.

These fundamental training concepts are needed to organize an effective puppy training program. Positive reinforcement is another crucial way to help your dogs gain your trust.

The Evolution of Dogs' Role and Perception

Your dog's predecessors didn't just serve as people's pets; long before they became the affectionate, sometimes combative, bed/couch hogs you love, they had other uses.

In the Ice Age

Dogs were more of a need than a luxury during this time. They served as sentinels to ensure the security of human campsites. They were the ideal guardians because of their ability to bark and wolf-like sense of danger. Humans didn't realize until much later that dogs could locate other animals thanks to their keen sense of smell. Thanks to this recent finding, dogs can now be used to track animals and assist their two-legged counterparts in food hunting,

In prehistoric Egypt

Dogs played a significant part in the life of the modern Egyptian populace.

Although their function at the time was restricted to security, they could safeguard much more than just the living. Adding dog statues assisted the deceased in the afterlife and discouraged robbers. Because the ancient Egyptians thought so highly of dogs, they included them, along with cats, in their religion. The most notable example of a dog deity is the god Anubis, shown with a dog's head on the tombs of monarchs who have passed away. Being a pet-loving society, the Egyptians were the first to penalize acts of cruelty towards dogs.

With the Romans and Greeks

The Greek and Roman emperors found dogs during their trade with the Egyptians, and they were adopted as a permanent part of the Greek nobility. Their dogs did not, however, enjoy the same royal treatment as they received in Africa because both countries were more competitive than the ancient Egyptians. The Molossian and the Laconian Hound are the two dog breeds the Greeks began to breed.

The Molossian dogs, the progenitors of modern Mastiffs, had great popularity during the reign of Alexander the Great. Because of the dogs' enormous size, strength, bravery, and cunning, Aristotle agreed they were the greatest canines for warfare. Conversely, the Spartanbred Laconian Hound was renowned for being slimmer, quicker, and more vicious than a traditional Mastiff.

The Greeks did, however, have a warm place for their canines despite using them in battle. The epic poem The Odyssey states that upon the hero's homecoming, only his dog recognized him. After waiting for his master for a long time, the devoted dog finally crawls to him and wails joyfully before passing away.

Conversely, the Romans held their dogs in higher regard. Remus and Romulus were the two founders of Rome, and it is said that a she-wolf found them and reared them until Remus was assassinated by his twin brother. The inventive Romans developed heavy leather collars studded with metal blades to keep other dogs from biting at the throats of the Mother of Rome's descendants, all to keep them safe. Dogs, though, had to work for a living at the time. They pulled carts full of building supplies alongside horses, oxen, and cattle.

Their fleas contributed to this, as they spread the bubonic plague. Dogs were consequently abandoned as pets. In addition, they were abandoned in the wild, where they were forced to hunt and consume corpses in packs. Aristocrats gave them another chance long later, and they used their innate hunting abilities to assist them in hunting wildlife and killing both small and large animals. According to historical accounts, Henry I owned 200 hounds that his huntsmen would raise, train, and take on hunting trips with the royal party. The common people could not utilize dogs to hunt for sustenance or enjoyment until the late 1700s.

In the Victorian era

Queen Victoria is among the most well-known dog lovers in history. She had always been devoted to dogs, and after her husband passed away in 1861, her love for these fluffy animals grew even stronger. She owned dogs of almost fifteen different breeds. Her readiness to free convicts during various jubilees—as long as they weren't found guilty of animal cruelty—further demonstrates her affection for animals.

With the Queen of England at their side, dogs achieved unprecedented prestige and even became status symbols in their own right. At the time, your dog choice would tell others if you were a real gentleman or lady or just someone attempting to move up the social scale. As a result, one could say that the Victorian era was the height of dog culture.

Chapter 3: Let's Get Down to Business: The Session Has Started

Putting Structure in Place and Organizing

After the school year starts, the teacher immediately takes the teachings seriously. It's time to get down to business after the kids have had time to acclimate to their teacher and the classroom.

Having a specific objective in mind before implementing any session is beneficial. Decide exactly what it is that you want your dog to learn and how you're going to get there. Give your action plan significant thought because it will decide the degree of success obtained.

Organization and structure are crucial. You have wasted valuable time and lost your dog's focus if you have to end the session because you can't find the ball you are teaching him to fetch. A successful lesson time requires both preparation and structure. Do what any competent teacher would do and continue with the lesson, postponing interruptions until after it's over, even if a buddy drops by or the phone rings.

Try your best to eliminate distractions for your dog if that is the case. Turn off the water if it bothers your dog to play in the backyard while you are training or frightening him. If a cat is walking around incessantly, wait for him to go, or if he is your cat, bring him inside until the end of the school day.

There will always be some diversions. While some can be disregarded or eliminated, others cannot. The secret is to apply common sense. If it's exceptionally hot or rainy, postpone class until the weather improves. Teach your dog to concentrate despite distractions if you live in a noisy neighborhood, and things won't improve.

Let the lessons begin now that your classroom and lesson plan are organized! There are several fundamental instructions that your dog has to learn, regardless of whether you are training your puppy or dog for obedience because of negative behavior that needs to be corrected or as a preventative measure. Even if your dog has some experience and is familiar with the fundamental commands, reviewing them as a refresher is still a good idea.

Basic Guidelines for Obedience:

Take a seat. Teaching your dog to sit is not only the first thing on the "A, B, C" chart when it comes to dog training, but it's also important for safety reasons. If your dog automatically sits when you ask him to, you can prevent him from going into situations where he could end up in danger or become a threat. Making him sit will also prevent him from bothering other people. This is possibly the most crucial lesson of all, so by all means, don't skip it. This four-step method will help you quickly teach your dog to sit and will mark a significant advancement in educating him to be obedient.

Step 1: Train Your Dog to Sit with Verbal Cues.

● You will begin this class by teaching by example. To begin, stand and give the signal to "Sit." Bring your dog to a sitting position with a gentle yet strong touch. Hold a reward with your other hand near your dog's nose, but keep it out of reach. Start lifting the treat so your dog chases it while maintaining a sitting position by sticking his nose high.

Try putting your dog in front of something, like a wall, if he retreats from the exercise. If he leaps to his feet, remind him to sit down.

● Give your dog affection, praise, and a treat when he finishes the assignment correctly.

● To ensure that your dog has understood the lesson, repeat it.

Step 2: Carry out the Lesson Again, but without the Treat.

● You will cup your hand as though you had a treat, even though this exercise doesn't require a treat to entice you. This is advantageous because your dog will be trained to follow your hand movements because it formerly contained a treat.

● Give your dog affection, praise, and a snack when he sits on cue.

Step 3 is to stop using the hand signal.

● Repeat the lesson, focusing just on the spoken cue.

● Show your dog a ton of love and affection, along with lots of praise and rewards when he obeys the command.

Step 4: Expand on the Lesson's Content.

It's time to train your dog to sit in certain areas on its initiative.

● To do this, take your dog through the lesson every time he comes into contact with someone, such as when you take him to visit a friend or when someone calls on your home. Mealtime is another good time to have your dog sit. Instruct him to sit while you fill his bowl, set it before him, and hold it until you take him out of the pose.

● To complete this mission, you must repeat the sit verbal cue whenever he sees a guest or someone for whom he is the guest and whenever he eats. It may take some time for some dogs to pick up this pattern, but perseverance is key, and ultimately, he will become proficient.

Lay down. Your dog is prepared to learn how to lie down once he has mastered sitting. It is taught in the same way, but it calls for a little more self-control because, in certain situations, such as when a lot is happening around him, he may be fine sitting but not comfortable lying down. However, this order is crucial. Even if he is not initially interested in the lesson, continue it because it can keep him safe and out of trouble. It is a significant rung on the ladder of excellent behavior.

● This lesson is rather easy, even though it might encounter some resistance. It's taught similarly to how you educate your dog to sit.

● Give your dog the instruction to "Lay Down," or just to "Lay" or "Down," while holding a goodie in one hand. Once more, you have complete control over the terminology you choose as long as you stay true to it.

● To assist your dog in falling asleep, gently press down on his hind legs and back until he is in the desired position. Next, give him a reward and some praise.

● After letting your dog get up, repeat the order with him, working on it until he gets it down pat.

● After your dog masters the cue, train him to stand again using "Up." Give your dog praise and rewards for a job well done.

VISUAL CONTACT

Making eye contact is essential to communicating. Puppies use their ability to visually interact with us to learn about our moods and what is happening in a given environment. Additionally, researchers have found that puppies can mimic our facial expressions and even decipher what they represent. Simply put, eye contact is gazing at someone like you would look at someone else. Looking at your lovely puppy's face and those dreaded "Puppy Dog Eyes" can make this difficult, but try not to give in to their cute appearance, keep to your strategy, and be assertive! When training your puppy, it's critical to understand the "training bubble," or the space between your eyes and theirs.

"Your puppy will react faster the closer you are with them."

You can reach your puppy's ideal eye level by starting eye contact training while seated on the ground. As time passes, you can start "stretching" that bubble and the space between you. If you try to do this too quickly, the bubble will burst.

HANDSIGNS

You will have to use a lot of hand gestures to communicate with someone you meet who does not speak your language. Puppies experience something similar. Hand gestures and nonverbal cues help communicate our message, even if kids won't fully comprehend all we say and may not even understand what we are saying from day one. For this reason, besides using words and assistance, you should gesture, point, and exaggerate your body language. Make sure to utilize a lot of non-verbal communication at first, but ultimately, the truth will come out, and you will know which one your puppy prefers. Some puppies respond better to hand signals than words, and vice versa. Please feel free to invent any hand gestures you like! Puppies can understand hand signals in a way that no other animal species can, so don't underestimate this ability.

According to Dr. Rabbit, "Indirect correlations among puppies and primates, puppies are more gifted at using human gestures to discover hidden objects or food."

For instance, he and other analysts found that, in contrast to chimpanzees, puppies would approach the right cup when two cups are presented, one with a treat placed beneath it, and they can then be encouraged to gaze at or point to it. Puppies are not allowed to use their sense of smell to find food; instead, they must follow hand gestures to locate the correct cup.

Reckless Dog
Stop Troublesome Conduct Before It Occurs.

Problem behavior in your newly acquired puppy is to be expected. Therefore, you should take care of it right away. At first, your new French Bulldog puppy just knows what comes naturally to him to survive. You must demonstrate to him what is appropriate and inappropriate. If you don't adequately discipline him, he won't learn why you are upset with him when he engages in inappropriate behavior and will continue with them as he ages. Unnecessary dog discipline verges on abuse, if not outright confusing and frightening for your pet.

Your French Bulldog puppy will also believe in his lovely head that he is the dominant dog if he suddenly turns dangerous when he gets older. This implies to him that he is free to disobey you. It won't be his fault either; instead, it will be your responsibility for not making him your Alpha Dog.

Suppose you went to the shelter and picked up an older, untrained dog instead of a puppy. He exhibits a lot of problematic behaviors. Well done for saving him. It's better for you to still establish power and teach him no.

Being too easy or rough on their dogs is a common mistake pet owners make. Generally speaking, severe physical punishment is never required.

Additionally, indulging your dog or ignoring bad actions's not a good idea. In order to create harmony between him and you as the Alpha, you must be firm but also gentle.

You have the right to refuse anything you don't like. Your dog's permissions are final regarding what he may and cannot do. Be the boss and take charge of him without fear. You just have to be mindful of him. Not yapping back.

Every breed of domesticated dog yearns for your guidance and the role modeling of Alpha. It's easier to train certain dogs than others. There are more obstinate dogs. Simply exercise patience and persistence in your training. You can only train your French Bulldog to understand your desires this way.

Furthermore, maintain consistency. If you reward your puppy or older dog for good behavior and ignore it at other times, you won't be able to train him to stop harmful behaviors.

Don't punish him for things he did in the past. He is not going to recall. Additionally, don't give him gifts or praise him after reprimanding him for ten minutes; otherwise, you will convey contradicting messages. Because he is such an adorable little puppy, you might want to console and coddle him if he is cowering and pouting after you say no but resist the urge. The secret is to always train with extreme firmness and consistency.

Always reward good behavior and discourage poor behavior. That is, in essence, dog training.

Appropriate Order

You should apply the following kind of appropriate punishment to your French Bulldog:

Dominance training: Use this technique to assert your authority over your puppy when he behaves aggressively or disobeys you. Dominance doesn't have to be established by violence or cruelty. This is the method. Grasp his muzzle with one hand and his muzzle in the other. Hold his head down while you stand over him. He will finally yield when he looks up at you or relaxes his body. Give him some praise and let go. To demonstrate authority without causing any discomfort, just pull tightly on your dog's scruff, which is the loose skin around his neck.

Refusing to Say No! A resounding "No!" can effectively teach your French Bulldog to be a good guy. Your voice will compel your dog to obey you when you are dominant. He shows you respect by listening to you and desiring what you say.

Time out: You can periodically put your dog in a time out where he will be sent away. It is not appropriate to misuse such a strong and significant punishment. Locate a quiet, uninteresting area, such as the porch, laundry room, or outside if there are no activities. Tell your dog to "Time out" and lead him to the designated area whenever he does something that is not permitted. If your dog can lie down or sit comfortably and won't choke or worse, tie him up on a shortened two-foot line or something similar. Give him a few minutes by yourself there. Tell him he's a good kid and release him when he's completely calmed down.

Positive Behavior: Teach positive behaviors to your French Bulldog. We shall discuss this topic in greater detail in later portions of this chapter. Essentially, the aim is to substitute negative habits with positive ones by teaching him. Give praise for any well-done actions. Tell him "No" and give him instructions to behave well instead of acting badly when he does something wrong. Barking from your dog is a good illustration of this. Teach him to stay quiet and assume that he will comply. Give him praise when he succeeds, and reprimand him when he fails. Teaching him positive behaviors is a fantastic method to model conduct for him.

Section Two

Comprehending THE SPECIALITIES OF THE BREED

The adaptable and energetic Wirehaired Pointing Griffon breed is renowned for their amiable disposition and hunting prowess. They are distinguished by a handful of distinctive traits unique to their breed.

First and foremost, they have an amazing appearance. They have a thick, protective undercoat and a coarse, wiry topcoat on a climate-safe double coat. Thanks to this distinctive coat, they can endure harsh terrain and weather patterns while maintaining their hunting advantage. They have a rugged yet endearing appeal due to their messy appearance.

In terms of temperament, Wirehaired Pointing Griffons are renowned for their friendly, affectionate, and want-to-please demeanor. They are highly trainable because of their innate wisdom and intense desire to collaborate closely with their owners. They are fantastic allies for vibrant individuals or families because of their innate energy and openness to learning.

They exhibit an extraordinary sense of smell and the innate ability to locate and retrieve games when hunting. They are invaluable to trackers, succeeding in various environments from upland fields to waterfowl bogs because of their keen sense of east from west and confidence in the field.

Since the outset, socialization has been essential for Wirehaired Pointing Griffons. They will typically thrive in environments with consistent training, mental stimulation, and more than enough exercise. Maintaining their look and health also requires regular maintenance, which includes brushing to prevent the matting of their distinctive coat.

Their devotion to their loved ones is one of their most notable traits. They form enduring relationships and recognize their importance to the family, thriving in camaraderie and cooperation with their fellow citizens. They are cherished family pets and excellent trackers due to their devotion and affectionate disposition.

The Wirehaired Pointing Griffon combines intelligence, affection, and a bit of roughness. Their distinctive coat, friendly nature, and exceptional hunting abilities make them a beloved breed for outdoor enthusiasts and families looking for a dependable and adaptable companion.

SETTING PURPOSE IN TRAINING

For wirehaired pointed Griffon training objectives, clarity, and regularity are essential. Keep your training sessions brief—roughly ten to fifteen minutes—to maintain their focus. *Positive reinforcement* is a powerful tool that uses friendship, treats, and praise to incentivize good behavior.

Include activities that make use of these active canines' innate senses. It's essential to teach them how to point and recover. To aid in their recuperation, start with simple fetch activities. Gradually introduce them to bird training if you plan to have them participate in hunting. Start with fictitious birds, and as they gain experience, switch to real ones.

Griffon socialization is crucial. Introduce children to various environments, people, and animals from the start. This avoids shyness or hostility. Use controlled cooperation to ensure that they develop positive behaviors around other people.

Follow a routine and exercise caution. Having redundancy helps reinforce actions and commands. Regular exercise bolsters your dog's training and strengthens your bond with him.

Setting reasonable goals is essential. Divide more ambitious projects into smaller, more manageable steps. For instance, start with basic compliance and gradually introduce them to scent trails and points if you have no desire to be a skilled tracker.

In the end, pay attention to their mental and physical stimulation. Griffons are energetic dogs that need cerebral challenges and physical exercise to thrive. Involve them in long walks, races, agility courses, or puzzle toys to keep them happy and active.

Remember that every dog is different, so modify your training regimen to fit your Griffon's personality and preferred learning style. Rejoice in victories and exercise patience when bad things happen. With dedication and a planned training schedule, your Wirehaired Pointing Griffon can develop into a talented, well-mannered buddy.

Section Five

Step Four

Step 4 looks at consistency, which is essential for successful housetraining.

Establishing a consistent training schedule and being patient when facing challenges are essential to ensuring your dog has a positive and productive learning experience.

Developing a Trustworthy Training Course

Maintaining consistency aids in teaching your dog expectations, which helps to stabilize and expedite the housetraining process. Establish a regular rest, play, feeding, and bathroom breaks schedule. Scheduling regularly reinforces the habit established in earlier steps, which helps your dog anticipate and respond to their needs.

When accidents happen, follow the recommended course of action without deviation. Just as important is consistency in response. Reward your dog for correct conduct and gently correct them if they stray from it. A more stable learning atmosphere results from consistent responses to wins and setbacks.

Overcoming Difficulties with Patience

Housetraining is a learning process that involves both you and your dog, and challenges are a common part of the journey. Overcome challenges with compassion and tolerance. Refrain from punishing or scolding your dog for misbehavior, which may increase their anxiety and hinder their learning ability.

Instead, focus on providing more guidance and praising positive behavior. If accidents begin to happen often, reevaluate your routine and adjust as necessary. Being patient when faced with challenges is crucial, and maintaining a calm and positive outlook ensures your dog develops in a nurturing atmosphere.

Maintaining consistency extends beyond the classroom. Ensure that any caregivers, including family members, who help with your dog's care follow the pattern and consistently respond to your dog's behavior. Together, we can solidify the knowledge gained and contribute to developing a well-mannered pet.

By the time this chapter ends, you will have a solid understanding of the importance of consistency in housetraining. Join us in Chapter 7, Problem-Solving and Troubleshooting, as we address common issues and provide practical troubleshooting tips. Your commitment to consistency lays the foundation for a positive housetraining experience for you and your pet.

Section Six

Step Number Five

You should be aware of and ready for a few common challenges before you begin housetraining. This chapter will look at effective problem-solving strategies and offer practical troubleshooting tips to give a more direct path to success.

Handling Common Housetraining Concerns

Since each dog is unique, housetraining can be challenging for each in different ways. The following section discusses some common obstacles that you may encounter:

Accidents indoors: If your dog continues to have accidents indoors, consider reviewing your routine and increasing the frequency of potty breaks. Ensure your dog gets many chances to relieve themselves in the designated area.

Reluctance to Crate Training: Some dogs may not agree to be housed in a. Gradually introduce your dog to the crate and encourage him to link it with safety and comfort by utilizing positive reinforcement. Make the crate a cheerful place by filling it with toys and snacks.

Fear of Outdoor Elements: Dogs may be reluctant to go outside in inclement weather. Go slowly, treat them, and commend them for their bravery as you adjust them to different weather conditions.

Marking Territory: Unneutered male dogs may leave markings on their territory. Reducing this habit can be helped by neutering. Healthy restroom habits should be rewarded with positive reinforcement.

The Annual Cost of Owning a Beagle

I

Let's talk about what influences the cost if you're considering obtaining a Beagle puppy or if you already have one and are wondering if the price is reasonable.

Yes, the upfront cost is significant, but don't overlook the continuing care costs. Things like where you live, where the puppy came from, how old the Beagle is, what kind of registration you choose, and how breeding limitations affect the total cost. We'll also clarify the subtleties by revealing why some pets are shockingly inexpensive or have exorbitant pricing.

Location and How It Affects Prices

Location is a major factor in potential costs, and it's not just about homes! The breeder's state greatly impacts how much Beagle puppies cost in the United States. However, there are no hard and fast guidelines for pricing; factors including supply, demand, and operating expenses all impact.

Most breeders are located in states with higher puppy birth rates.

For instance, compared to certain southern regions, there aren't as many Beagle breeders in the nation's northeastern region. Because fewer

Beagle pups are available, costs may be a little higher if you discover a tiny home breeder up north.

Many of them obtain their puppies from unsavory establishments known as puppy mills. Being a home-based dog breeder isn't a money-making venture. After paying for food, veterinary care, nice dogs, and other expenses, there is a tiny profit.

Exercise caution while selecting a breeder. While some are morally upright, others are just backyard breeders trying to turn a profit soon.

If you cannot locate a puppy in your state and must search outside, remember that shipping will increase the price. Whether you go fetch them or the pup flies to you, it may be expensive. A quality AKC registered Beagle puppy from a small home breeder typically costs more than one from a place with abundant puppies.

Cheap Prices

Is it accurate to say that you receive what you pay for?"

Well, not in every case. Puppy mills that produce puppies are still in operation in some areas. They flood the market with cheap puppies by selling them at flea markets, online, and pet stores.

This puts moral breeders in a difficult position because, in order to compete with these mills, they frequently have to maintain low prices. But some avaricious mills simply maintain high prices because they can.

The idea is that a Beagle's quality cannot be determined solely by price.

Influence of Seasons

Let's move on to discuss how pricing can change with the seasons.

Most individuals bring home new puppies in June and July in locations where the weather fluctuates. In order to select the ideal puppy from a litter, make a deposit, and prepare for the new furry family member, they begin looking in April and May.

It's the perfect time of year, with children off from school, adults taking time off to look after the dog, and pleasant weather that makes housebreaking less difficult.

But from November to March, things are different; snow, ice storms, and bitterly cold weather make it difficult to take a Beagle puppy home. Because there is less demand in the winter, many breeders take a break, which drives down prices. If you choose to get a Beagle in the "off-season," remember that inclement weather and snowfall may make training and maintenance more difficult.

How Price Changes with Age

An important factor in Beagle puppy pricing is time. Reputable breeders may require deposits for future litters, but the price normally decreases as the puppies reach eight weeks of age. A common misconception is that a puppy should be two months old when it is acquired. Therefore, it will probably be less expensive if the puppy is 9, 10, or 11 weeks old and hasn't been sold.

Find a reliable breeder and accept a little older dog. Adopting a retired Beagle is an additional choice. By the age of seven, or occasionally even younger, female Beagles stop breeding. At this stage, some are given new residences.

The cost can be cut in half if a person is willing to take on an older dog, and it's a terrific way to avoid the potty training stage and have a Beagle well-versed in commands.

An Immediate Overview Of Dog Training

That modifies a dog's behavior by using the natural events of its ancestors and outcomes. It is an exercise that facilitates the dog's effort at specific tasks or errands and its ability to participate successfully in modern local life. Dogs have been trained for specialized tasks since the Roman era. However, the 1950s suburbanization brought about the training of dogs to be good family pets.

A dog benefits from every interaction it has with its surroundings. It may occur through established conditioning, which creates a bond between two stimuli, or through non-cooperative realization, which modifies the dog's behavior by taming or sensitization. It can also be done using operant conditioning, which establishes a connection between an earlier event and its result.

Animal training regimens come in various forms, each with its followers and critics. The Koehler system, clicker method, strength-based training, negative support, and relationship-based training are some of the most well-known dog training techniques. Knowledge of the animal's characteristics and identity, discipline, consistent communication, and precise timing of reinforcement are all hallmarks of good training techniques.

The most loyal friends who can provide you with love and comfort are dogs. We have seen numerous news reports and read numerous amazing tales in books about how a pet dog saves its owner's life from various accidents and dangers. Dogs are highly intuitive; they can sense danger and bark to alert you. Still, your dog must be fully trained before it can understand your appearance and cues. Remember that dogs cannot understand human language, so the only methods of training they can receive are simple gestures and reward systems. I would suggest getting a puppy if you want another dog for a pet. It's beneficial because pups are easier to teach and should join your team once you've properly prepared them.

For any family dog, proper training is essential so that you can grasp their problems, and they should understand your movements. You must realize your dog only understands what you're signaling and doing. What you say to him doesn't concern him.

Whether you yell at him or whisper in his ears, "Jasmine—which might be the name of your pet—come here!" has no bearing on the situation. All he has to do is understand your gestures and body language. Therefore, it is necessary to ingrain this concept into your mind before providing appropriate preparation. Ways include using clickers, engaging in physical activities, teaching hand and body signals, and many more. We should become familiar with some standard guidelines so that you can begin training your dog as soon as possible.

As a result, I wrote this book by considering any dog's general approach. It makes no difference if they are German Shepherds, Chihuahuas, Bulldogs, or any other breed you own. That said, I guarantee you will find this book to help train your dog.

There are a few misconceptions regarding dog training. Dog trainers employ different methods and intensities of instruction when teaching a dog. You will feel differently after speaking with trainers, reviewing their websites, and reading testimonials from friends and former clients. Although the internet has proven to be a fantastic teaching tool, it has also helped spread many false beliefs about training puppies. Here are a few of the more common ones you might encounter while looking for a dog training tutor.

Myth: A dog is either hard-headed, overbearing, stupid, or a combination of all three if he cannot take in behavior.

As regards the misconception above, dogs and people are indeed very similar. Some dogs can move objects quickly, while others need more time and guidance. Often, when we as mentors observe a puppy having trouble running an errand, the dog isn't being trained in a way that the dog understands. Occasionally, they fail to complete an errand because they are not properly taught. Additionally, because of the way the training has been carried out, there is no possibility that the dog will understand what you are asking of them. Consistently reward your dog when they perform well. Additionally, you want to exhibit tolerance in your dog's behavior.

If your puppy still doesn't seem to be able to learn anything new and practical, take a moment to reflect on your training methods from the dog's standpoint. Consider the possibility that some behaviors may not be as clearly taught as you believed, or maybe elements of the surroundings are. It is so complex that it cannot be broken down into smaller steps, perhaps due to needs. It's also reasonable to consider whether the dog is physically capable of engaging in a particular behavior. For example, a dog with hip problems might struggle to "sit" down.

Myth: My dog appears blameworthy because he understands he did something wrong.

Reality: Animals can feel guilt in the same ways as humans, although scientists disagree on this point quite a little. Regarding the "liable look," however, a recent study conducted at New York's Barnard College discovered that the reason behind a person's "suspect look" at their dog is their response. There is a two-way flow depending on whether the person is expected to see the look in the animal.

Regardless of whether their pet had done something to warrant "blameworthy" consequences, they would simply ignore it. When dogs appear "blameworthy," they react to a shift in our nonverbal cues that informs them that "something isn't right." This causes the dog to exhibit nonverbal cues that, to an observer, appear anxious and agitated. The puppy has learned how to exhibit these behaviors by remembering that the ultimate purpose is to placate those who exhibit irrational nonverbal communication.

Getting Ready for the Dog

One of the most fulfilling experiences you can ever have is becoming a pet owner, but you must be prepared! Your family and you will have already discussed the type of dog you want to bring into your house. Your surroundings will greatly influence your choice of breed. You might lean toward a larger dog if your home has a vast space that can be used for exercise; on the other hand, if you live in an apartment, a smaller breed might be more appropriate.

Exercise plays a major role in a dog's lifestyle, and if a regular walking plan is established early in the day, it will prevent many disagreements. This organizing technique may be used for every element of your new pet's care, and your home will benefit your new pet if you decide which family members will do which tasks.

Spend some time compiling a list of words used with your dog. Reducing confusion will make your training far more effective and your dog happier. Ensure everyone interacting with your new pet understands and adheres to the important phrases for your new addition.

You must shop before you get a puppy! Water and food bowls, toys, bedding, a collar and leash, a dog crate, and an ID tag are among the needed supplies. Of course, many more products are available to produce a spoiled dog, but until you truly know your pet's personality, try to stay with the essentials! If you're adopting a puppy, investing in some excellent odor-neutralizers and puppy pads could be worthwhile. You can shop around and visit the trendy new pet retailer without stressing that your dog needs it immediately if you finish shopping before your new friend arrives.

Whatever the age of your new pet, you will need to set up the room in your house where it will spend the next few months as its home. To make things easier for both of you, decide where your pet will sleep and spend most of its time. You should also take some preventative measures. To prevent mishaps, tape unsecured electrical lines to baseboards, remove all breakables from the area, and possibly move any valuable rugs out of the way. After you are certain that everything has been completed, lie down on the ground for a moment and consider things from your new dog's point of view!

The eager new owners may begin now that the house has been resolved! Despite the allure of creating a commotion, ensure everyone knows the importance of not overindulging your new pet. Your new addition will just become confused and overexcited by you. You must be consistent from the start. Inquire as to when and what Fido was fed last, and for the first few days, stick to that schedule. It wouldn't be a good start for either of you to have gastric distress. Dietary adjustments and feeding schedules should be made gradually over several weeks.

Fundamental Training in Obedience

Having a well-behaved dog is a pleasure. Dogs need boundaries; they are happier and more content when they know what is expected of them. Utilizing fundamental obedience training techniques and being aware of your dog's reactions will help you prevent bewilderment and anxiety, which frequently result in scared pets who can later grow into dangerous ones.

Recognize the learning process of dogs.

Dogs live in the present moment; you must understand that. Returning home to a house covered in torn pillows and excrement all over the floor is possible. Your dog will never be able to link the mess you discovered to any punishment you administer. While it may be annoying, shouting at your dog will make them confused and afraid. You cannot teach your dog to behave this way after the fact. Only by observing canines in the act can you correct the behavior.

Give behaviors repercussions.

In other words, appropriate behavior should be rewarded, and inappropriate behavior should be appropriately addressed. Teach your dog that good behavior will result in positive reinforcement. Make sure you always have treats on hand, and when Fido acts like the collected, easygoing dog that we all want to see, give it a pat and a treat. Treats and attention are two of a dog's favorite things and are quite easy to please.

Likewise, yelling and shouting down undesirable behavior is not the appropriate way to deal with it. Dogs do not comprehend English; therefore, they will only become agitated and afraid that their pack leader is losing control. This is why your dog does not understand why you are making loud noises and becoming angry. The best thing to do is to ignore Fido when he is acting out, like jumping up and getting too enthusiastic. When you ignore negative behavior, your dog will quickly learn that it will make them feel excluded and cease acting out.

Your best buddy is consistency!

When teaching, it's critical to be consistent with your dog's consequences. When your dog leaps on you, and you walk away, but your spouse finds it cute and gives Fido cuddles and encouragement, that dog will expect positive attention from anyone who comes to the house, so he will jump up whenever they do. When training your pet, everyone in your home must act the same way. When rewarding good behavior, timing is also crucial; your pet has to know precisely which conduct resulted in positive responses.

Teaching your dog that a good thing will happen whenever the signal appears is the first step in using signals with him. Using a clicker—a basic hand-held device that produces a noise your dog will eventually come to identify with a reward—is one way to train your dog through positive reinforcement. Additionally, you can use your voice to encourage your pet. Just saying "good" or "well done" optimistically can let him know that his behavior has pleased you.

Enjoy yourselves!

Like anything else, teaching your dog should be enjoyable. Otherwise, it will show! Limit the length of your training sessions and concentrate on just one or two abilities at a time. Remember that while dogs all learn best through repetition, they do so at different rates. Decide on a session length and begin the schedule with the first skill you want to teach Fido. Repeat this several times before moving on to anything else. Continue repeating this until your dog gets bored or you've used up all the time allocated!

Setting priorities for your training methods will be easier when you realize that mastering simple obedience techniques will enhance overall behavior. When your pet learns to sit and remain, you can train him to respond differently to other triggers, like the doorbell or visitors. Better responses in various situations can result from this one behavioral adjustment.

How to Be Ready for Your Dachshund

How to Proof Your Home for Puppies

Make sure your house is puppy-proof before bringing a dachshund puppy home. Their small size and inquisitive attitude allow them to fit into various nooks and crevices. Here are some suggestions for dachshund puppy proofing:

- Get to know your puppy. Examine the spaces beneath and surrounding furniture to determine what they may access. If a space exists, dachshunds can squeeze in under bookcases and appliances.

- Keep hazardous areas off. To prevent your pet from getting hurt or coming into contact with anything toxic, use baby gates to restrict access to areas like the kitchen, laundry room, and garage. If you have steps, you must have stair gates.

- Cut off any loose wires. Avoid allowing your dog to chew on electrical lines, which could lead to electrocution. Place cord coverings on your purchases or tuck them behind furniture.

- Lockable garbage cans. Trash has many enticing smells and might be dangerous for pups. Put wastebaskets in closed cupboards your dog cannot open, or use cans with locking lids.

- Fit locks on cabinets. Dachshunds are skilled surfers of kitchen counters. Put child-proof latches on lower cabinets to prevent your pet from reaching the cabinets.

- Fasten doors and drawers. Lock up dresser drawers, closet doors, entertainment units, etc., to prevent curious dogs from becoming stuck inside.

- Gather indoor plants. Numerous common houseplants pose a risk to dogs. Move them out of reach or look at safe options for dogs.

- Eliminate any trip hazards. To prevent falling on your low-lying dog, pick up any loose items such as books, blankets, cords, shoes, etc.

Examine the yard. Before allowing your dachshund to wander, walk around the yard and look for any hazards, such as jagged branches, poisonous plants or mushrooms, or gaps in the fence that need fixing.

- Establish a secure area. While you're at work, set up an exercise pen or a safe, puppy-proof room where your dachshund is welcome to spend time to prevent boredom and provide toys.

- Be ready for mishaps. Paper towels, stain/odor removers, and pet-safe cleansers will be useful for those inevitable potty training mishaps. Assign a designated outdoor restroom.

- Invest in gates and barriers. You can limit access with additional x-pens, baby gates, and ex-pens until manners and housetraining improve. Prevent entry to off-limits areas.

Take the time to thoroughly dog-proof your house in advance. Nothing in this world should be overlooked. Keep a watchful eye on things your dachshund tries to chew on or shows interest in inspecting and replacing them. In the long run, puppy-proofing safely pays off!

List of Supplies to Buy

A dachshund puppy requires specific equipment and supplies to be added to your home. Before they arrive, be ready with these essential items for dachshund puppies:

- Crate: A wire crate with a dividing panel makes a comfortable haven for unwinding. It also stops destruction and helps with potty training.

Bedding: Give your dog comfortable places to sleep with fleece blankets, washable bed linens, and plush crate cushions. They can go between rooms because there are multiple beds.

- Bowls: Sturdy bowls made of stainless steel that resist chipping and toppling. Think about slow-feed bowls to cut down on scarfing. Additionally, bowls are available in heights that may be adjusted to suit long-bodied dachshunds.

- Collar + leash - A lightweight collar and a 4-6 foot leash are essential for walks, tags, and lead control. Choose supple materials to prevent your long-coat dachshund's fur from matting.

- ID tag: If your pet gets lost, tags engraved with your contact information give you peace of mind that they can be found. Since collar tags jingle, dachshunds should always wear breakaway tags when left alone.

- poop bags + scooper - Bring plenty of bags to pick up after poop on walks.

Keep a special poop scooper on hand for easy cleanup of the restroom.

- Grooming supplies: To keep your dachshund's coat tidy, use a wire slicker brush, comb, nail clippers, and shampoo made specifically for dogs. Longhairs require more extensive grooming supplies.

- Toys - Your energetic dog will get mental and physical exercise from interactive toys, including food puzzles, pull ropes, balls, and squeaky toys. To maintain their interest, rotate.

Snacks: Soft snacks enhance training and promote positive behavior. Search for small-breed or puppy-formulated treats that your dachshund could enjoy nibbling on.

- Cleaning supplies: During the potty training phase of a puppy, pet-safe cleansers, spot removers, paper towels, etc. will be quite useful.

- Baby gates: These help with supervision around the house by limiting access to areas that haven't been puppy-proofed. They are an essential safety tool.

Food and water dishes: Flat-bottomed, shallow bowls designed specifically for brachycephalic (smush-faced) dogs are a good way to keep food from coming into contact with dachshund ears.

- X-pen/gates: With these portable setups, you may establish a secure area or restrict access to specific house areas for educational and monitoring purposes.

Make sure to cross everything on your list well in advance of the arrival of your dachshund. Preparing and setting up the puppy for their big first day home is much easier when everything is ready.

www.ingramcontent.com/pod-product-compliance
Lightning Source LLC
Chambersburg PA
CBHW052135110526
44591CB00012B/1735